PARABLES OF THE BIBLE

PARABLES OF THE BIBLE
The Son Who Came Home

Drejervej 15,3 DK-2400 Copenhagen NV, Denmark
Tel.: (+45) 3531 0330 Fax: (+45) 3531 0334
E-mail: info@scanpublishing.dk
Website: www.scanpublishing.dk

Design by Ben Alex
Printed in China
ISBN 87 7247 782 2 (Hard cover)
ISBN 87 7247 778 4 (Soft cover)

PARABLES OF THE BIBLE

THE SON WHO CAME HOME

Luke 15:11—32

Illustrations by
Gustavo Mazali

scandinavia

A sad father

Once there was a man who had two sons. One day, the younger son told his father he wanted to leave home. He also asked his father to give him a lot of money. The father gave it to him and sadly said goodbye.

Bad friends

The son traveled to a land far away. There he used his father's money on foolish things and spent time with bad friends who did things he knew were wrong.

All alone

Now the son had spent all his father's money, and his bad friends had left him. He was all alone, with no money to buy food. So he got a job taking care of pigs. He was so hungry he even ate the pigs' food.

The son goes home

Finally the son decided he would go back to his father and ask forgiveness. He would offer to work hard for his father and even become a servant. He thought he was no longer good enough to be treated as a son.

The father welcomes his son

The father was waiting at home. As soon as he saw his son coming, he ran out and hugged him.

"I forgive you, son," he said. "Come in and let's have a homecoming party!"

The father still loved the son, no matter what he had done.

A homecoming party

The father was very happy. He told his servants to prepare a feast for his son.

"My son was lost, but now he has come home again!" he said.

The son who came home

—read the story in the Bible

"There was a man who had two sons. The younger one said to his father, 'Father, give me my share of the estate.' So he divided his property between them.

"Not long after that, the younger son got together all he had, set off for a distant country and there squandered his wealth in wild living. After he had spent everything, there was a severe famine in that whole country, and he began to be in need. So he went and hired himself out to a citizen of that country, who sent him to his fields to feed pigs. He longed to fill his stomach with the pods that the pigs were eating, but no one gave him anything.

"When he came to his senses, he said, 'How many of my father's hired men have food to spare, and here I am starving to death! I will set out and go back to my father and say to him: Father, I have sinned against heaven and against you. I am no longer worthy to be called your son; make me like one of your hired men.' So he got up and went to his father.

"But while he was still a long way off, his father saw him and was filled with compassion for him; he ran to his son, threw his arms around him and kissed him."

Luke 15:11-20